WHERE THE HELL DID I PARK MY LIFE?!

OWNER'S MANUAL FOR SHIFTING YOURSELF FORWARD

KAARI ALLEN M.A.

Where The Hell Did I Park My Life? Owner's Manual For Shifting Yourself Forward

Photo Credits: John Allen (city image cover); Kaari Allen; Susan Murphy; Robert Doyle

Images from Pixabay Artists HardyS from Pixabay; Gerd Altmann; Gaertringen; Antonio Doumas; Wokandapix; congerdesign; Markus Distelrath; Andrew Martin; Gordon Johnson. Adobestock (parking lot image-cover)

Printed in the United States of America

ISBN: 978-1-946195-43-2

23 22 21 20 19 5 4 3 2 1

Cover Design & Interior Book Design: Ann Aubitz

Published by FuzionPress - 1250 E 115th Street, Burnsville, MN

Dedication

To every reader and every person, I hope that you will always be moving forward.

Acknowledgments

John Allen, thank God I waited for you! You swept me off my feet, carried me, walked beside me and made me whole. You are an amazing man and I love you unconditionally.

Ben Allen, you are one in 1 million! It's one of the greatest joys of my life to love you and to play a part along with your parents.

Mom and Dad, well you know who you are and what you mean to me. Thank you for always being who and how you are to all of us.

Susan Murphy, you are the wind beneath my wings.

Rolf S., the partnership in all things "life" has and always will be priceless.

Craig M., thanks for "making" me put my thoughts to paper somehow, someway, around a bonfire at Camp ... or otherwise. Your wisdom and friendship are a gift.

Kathy H. and Vicki F., you are incredible healers as well as human beings. The world needs more you, for this I am certain.

Adrian, Karen and Charlie you created a "nest" and a safe place for me to be in this world. I wouldn't be breathing without you!

Joe S., Cindy B.& Grayce B.Y., thank you for believing in me and providing friendship as well as a launching pad.

Dr. Walsh, Dr. Falconer, Nikki H., and Peggy N., you are healers and thanks for not being totally sick of me or (at least pretending you aren't).

Denise T. you protect me and advocate for the truth, I am forever grateful.

Melanie B. and Jack U., you offered me a path with guidance and courage.

Dear God, there were many times that I was pretty ticked off at you and scared. Thank you for never allowing me to know how the chapters of my life thus far would unfold as everything you orchestrate is always in all our best interests. Always.

Table of Contents

FORWARD SHIFT		|9
CHAPTER 1	DISAPPOINTMENT TO DELIGHT	|13
CHAPTER 2	ONE THING CHANGES... EVERYTHING!	|21
CHAPTER 3	MY CHECKING ACCOUNT HAS $1.48 IN IT	|33
CHAPTER 4	EATING ICE CREAM FOR BREAKFAST	|39
CHAPTER 5	I NEVER REALLY LIKED PIE ANYHOW...	|41
CHAPTER 6	YOU CAN'T MOVE FORWARD USING ONLY ONE OAR	|57
CHAPTER 7	SKI WEAR AND PAJAMAS	|63
CHAPTER 8	I GET TO VS I HAVE TO	|73
CHAPTER 9	MAKE SURE TO CELEBRATE YOUR BELLY	|81
CHAPTER 10	LIKE IT OR NOT...	|89
CHAPTER 11	ELEMENTARY SCHOOL FIELD DAY LIVING UP OR DOWN TO EXPECTATIONS	|97
CHAPTER 12	YOU DESERVE A BREAK EVERYDAY	|107
CHAPTER 13	PAINT THAT PIG AND LET YOUR LIGHT SHINE	|115
CHAPTER 14	THE POTATOES WERE A COMPLETE DISASTER	|125
CHAPTER 15	WELCOME TO LIFE FUNERAL CELEBRATIONS	|133
CHAPTER 16	THE PEN IS MIGHTIER THAN THE TEXT/EMAIL	|143
CITATIONS		|153

Forward Shift

Looking back, both of my hands had become numb, as had my soul.

This reality hit me just when I thought that I had finally gotten my proverbial *"ducks in a row"*. I'd been thinking that all my striving, working and achieving was somehow going to reward me with the tangible and coveted gold medal in the "**Life Olympics**".

Damnit, it didn't happen.

Peeking over my shoulder, as scary as that was, I was aghast at not seeing even one duck at least attempting to waddle in a row behind me. (Exactly how many ducks does a legitimate row constitute anyhow? Someone really should research this mysteriously elusive number of ducks that warrants us having our *@#%! together and report back to the rest of us, soon.)

With my numb hands attached to my numb soul, I continued to carry on killing myself at work and life .... up to now. For many years, the way my desk and keyboard in my office/classroom were positioned cut off the circulation to my hands. Too busy to really pay attention to the tingling feeling, this mimicked a kink in a hose with barely the drip, drip, drip of water coming out. My head was disconnected from my body, and I cared about the kids and sorted responsibilities at the school too much to stop and truly listen to my body and my heart.

After twenty-seven years in the classroom as a special education teacher, diagnostician, trainer and presenter, I had to accept that this non-ergonomic workstation in my office was a messenger from God, the Universe, my Guardian Angel, or simply a gigantic billboard in front of me that read *"You MUST shift something NOW" because this is negatively shifting you without your permission nor your blessing."*

Not *could I, or should I*. Not a recommendation or a *maybe*, but *"Kaari, your body is telling you there is no other option!" Period, the end.*

Six surgeries, the retraining of my hands, a Staph infection and the loss of a career culminated in the grand finale ... an "exhaustive break down" (which meant that I was hauled off on a stretcher in an ambulance to a trauma, mental health unit at a local hospital to 'Time Out' for a week). The discharge papers prescribed this: *"Patient must continue to medically manage her adrenal fatigue and seek ongoing professional help for her exhaustion."*

The patterns by which I had previously lived had to shift to ensure my safety and sanity. Guess I had no choice at 48 yrs. old but to sit on my hands and hope that those little ducks of @#&%! would show up on my doorstep requesting a do-over, and be lined up neatly in a row. Half of my life had been lived, but not necessarily "living". There really could be a new life in the second half.

Somehow, I needed to be present, "out there" in the world, but in a very different way.

Life is ridiculously challenging at times. It is also unbelievably rewarding, invigorating and healing if we allow ourselves to shift our perspective a bit in response to **everyday circumstances**. Quite frankly, aren't we all simply buffoons on a bus headed to who knows where just trying to figure out how to **BE** in this life?

My altered hand warranted hiring someone to kick my butt and type my ideas for me to start a new life "out there". This someone showed up in the form of Susan Murphy, a marketer and gracious woman who encouraged me to blog. What? Who? Me? Really, I have something to share after surviving to this point due to the self- imposed approaches I had taken thus far? Ironic huh? These *Someone's* also included my amazing husband John.

Full disclosure, I didn't even know where to start, what to say or how to say it. However, the shifts manifested. This book reflects those shifts that propelled me forward. I created the activities included as well as adding opportunities for reflection, doodling or however you choose to utilize this. This is **YOUR** book not mine. May it serve you in any way you see fit for your heart and soul. Maybe, just maybe, it may shift you forward, keep you going, or at the very least, make you laugh and stir up some hope in your heart.

With every wish for a life you adore and deserve,

Kaari

1

Disappointment to Delight

Let it go or be dragged

Prior to the dawn of present-day Hand-Held-Headaches that rule our communication superhigh-ways, there was the answering machine. You may remember that coveted black box of old that held so much power. It not only offered recorded messages conveying pertinent information, but also affected how allegedly popular or unpopular we felt. *"You have three unheard messages,"* the recorded voice would say after pushing the blinking red button. Mind you, without the yet-to-be-invented clairvoyance of the Caller ID, the anticipation of who and what ruled us. *"End of messages,"* the mechanical voice would say.

He never called that night back in 1994. I waited all evening, jumping up every time the phone would ring. He said he would call, so I believed he would. I eventually gave up at midnight and went to bed in tears.

For many of us, we've been disappointed too many times to count throughout our lives. We didn't get an invite to that HUGE birthday party in sixth grade. After working at a particular company busting our butts, we've been passed over for the promotion. We didn't make the sports team or a relative or close friend let us down. Tell you what, not having anyone to sit with at lunch in junior high sure shook my world.

(This kind of disappointment in a kid's formative years breaks my heart for any child. I will get off my soapbox, but it just flat out hurts.) There is absolutely no warranted reason that we can see, nor something that could have been done or changed to alter the outcome; it just happened. Insert gut punch here…

All of these events are disappointing at best, life-altering at worst. Great, but now what?

Describe a disappointment

"If we will be quiet and ready enough, we shall find compensation in every disappointment."
-Henry David Thoreau

It takes a butt-load of courage to move forward so that disappointment can lead to discovery and development. And when we reflect, it can lead to discernment, determination and even delight. Delight from disappointment!?

Before you want to send me nasty notes or light this page on fire, please bear with me and read on.....

When a physical injury I sustained on the job led to a heartbreaking disappointment in my former teaching role, everything changed, EVERYTHING. Not being there, after years of being surrounded by students and colleagues, many of whom became dear friends, damaged my sense of ingrained identity and truly rocked my world. The first Monday morning of the following school year I woke up with no meeting to attend, nowhere that I HAD to be, and I simply didn't know what the hell to do. It felt like a vacuum had sucked the life and breath right from my soul.

So, in some half-hearted attempt to move forward, I went to a yoga class at 9 a.m. that morning. Sure, my hand was in a brace and I didn't necessarily fit in with those ladies in the locker room. For starters, I wasn't in what was my old uniform - a skirt, pointy heels and pearls. Oh, and of course the school issued lanyard with the ID hanging around my neck was missing. I just brought my yoga mat and me. Hell, I didn't even have any cute yoga clothes nor work out gear. You know, the kind that match and provide you the instant athletic costume. I guessed that the women in the locker room must have had prospective husbands or partners (assumed breadwinners) and children of their own that were in school. I felt out of my body as "just me". Don't get me wrong, my own personal life was and still is, wonderful in my role as wife and a step-mom; it simply looked and felt nothing like theirs. The loneliness of my post-disappointment rebuilding and discovering chapter was nothing short of scary and overwhelming. Back then, not even my husband nor my dogs really knew what I was doing while I was out. At least if you don't show up at the office on a given day, your co-workers would alert the authorities to confirm your whereabouts and well-being.

I had no office to show up at.

I was dying inside. There is no course such as *"The Disappointment Recovery Retreat"* you can take online that includes some workbook to enable recovery. For weeks, I would strategically place my mat in the darkest corner of the back row of the yoga studio. Slowly tumbling, not just in my body, but in my heart. I didn't realize it then that not only would things never be the same, they could be even better!

Our disappointments or so-called 'discoveries' remind us that what used to be is not really what's BEST for us. In the long run, these unanticipated, negative events open space, time and energy. The job opportunity that is no longer, the boyfriend or girlfriend who broke up with us, or the client who suddenly decided not to hire us have all prospectively freed up the time, space and energy for the momentum to shift and force us to grow.

After attending Harvard's Learning and The Brain Conference years ago, I heard a speaker share this:

"We can't alter the hard wiring of our brains but we can physiologically and emotionally free up space. The human brain is capable of being malleable and open to change throughout our entire life span."

We can free up our brain's and soul's bandwidth. Think of your lifespan as one delicious recipe - disappointments and all. There is time to marinate it, season it with different ingredients, and serve it with various side dishes i.e. events, people, life changes. There is also an ever-changing dessert menu as well as an ever-changing wine list to accompany us, always.

Don't discourage, don't remain dragged down... just continue to pull up a chair to the table of development. Trust me, it really is delicious.

SHIFT

It hurt when…

I realized that…

____

____

____

____

____

____

____

____

____

____

____

____

____

____

____

____**!!!**

2

One Thing Changes...

EVERYTHING!

Yes, there's change beyond hair color, underwear, and socks.

"Each day is an opportunity to make even just ONE change for the better. The blessing is that, at the end of each day, we have the chance to try something new tomorrow."

IT happened for me before yoga class that most eye-opening day. Mind you, I still can't take part in many of the yoga poses because of my altered hand. Yet, I soon discovered that simply laying on the mat would prove to be just as awe-inspiring. Hard for me to just lay there, really.

Change was imposed (lovingly of course) on all of us in class. Our instructor told us to move our individual yoga mats from the sacred spot that each of us had selected and be ready to change places.

WHAT?! Yeah, I know, can you believe it? I am always on the right side of the room in the corner; now <u>this</u>? Change? Switch places? *Honestly, I think I would have rather been injected with a series of rabies shots right there in the class.*

Speaking for myself, I always sit in the same place in a classroom, dinner table or church pew. Yup, same parking spot at the mall or workplace. Every time. It could be a senior moment thing, or I am just a creature of habit. Don't get me started sharing the horrors of looking for my car when I park somewhere different, heaven forbid. Aren't those radio frequency key fobs great? They not only unlock your car but they also locate it <u>for</u> you with sound and blinking lights. Somehow, our ancestors figured it out without these modern-day conveniences. Just sayin'.

After having my mini-hyperventilation moment in class that morning and living to tell about it, our instructor proceeded to direct us to meet someone new in class and then physically change places with that person. I do love what he said next;

"If we change one thing, we change EVERYTHING."

Taking a moment or two to process his declaration as well as not breaking into hives, I pondered how simply changing places and meeting someone new changed something IN me. One thing we do know 'for sure' (and there aren't many 'for sures' in our world today), is that nothing remains the same. Nothing. Change is part of the fabric of all our lives, minute by minute, day after day, year after year.

Our reliable friend Merriam Webster Dictionary defines change:

1. To become different
2. To make (someone or something) different
3. To become something else

Don't those options sound good? By simply doing something differently we garner information; a better way in which to live our lives or add joy and fulfillment. And yet, we don't learn a darn thing until we change our behavior.

Change can constitute any number of things: something small like using a new laundry detergent, or something big such as a job change. Change could be a new and modified perspective you may have, a different awareness of something or someone. You could change living arrangements or start a brand-new relationship. What about taking a new path to work? When I drive an unfamiliar route to my office or take the proverbial scenic route to go anywhere, it is just that – SCENIC! Think about it, to see something different allows us to experience more of the world. Nine times out of ten, I find myself saying" Hmmm, never knew there was a lake there." Or "This way is longer, but I feel calmer and enjoy it more."

Call me crazy, but these small changes are free. Free, as in zero dollars, $0.

Just there for the taking.

Anything we do to change even the slightest of things in our prospective worlds can open windows of opportunity and growth. It can propel us to learn something new or more importantly, alter our perspective about life.

> ***"Growth is painful. Change is painful. But nothing is more painful as remaining stuck somewhere you don't belong."***
> **-N.R. Narayana Murthy[1]**

In our lives, it matters not what situation we are in, or whether the circumstances of our lives are up or down, we have CHOICE. We always have choice.

The human brain has an amazing capacity to take in information, make sense of it and then apply it to the pertinent situation. From an academic perspective, this is called our working memory. I won't belabor the science, but working memory is worth noting. We don't want to lose sight of, and more importantly forget to <u>celebrate</u> the amazing, malleable nature of our brain as it serves as Mission Control over our individual lives.

What have you done differently lately, big or small?

____

____

____

____

____

____

____

How did it feel?

____

____

____

____

____

____

____

____

____

____

____

A change I have made you may ask? This was a much-needed adjustment let me add, yikes. Rushing out the door awhile back, I left the house wearing only one hoop earring. *Is the Pirate Look still in, Matey? Help Me.*

I wasn't rushing because I was late. I just didn't take the time to put the other earring in. Seriously. Not taking the time to put in the other earring? There ARE only 2. How long would that have taken; oh, I don't know, MAYBE 3 seconds tops?

I drove down the road and after looking in the mirror and suddenly realizing that I had only one hoop earring on it hit me - the absurdity of this rushing thing had to stop. Something had to change. I needed to make the choice to consciously begin downshifting and decelerating the pace at which I move through life.

As the legendary Lily Tomlin famously quipped,

"Whether or not you win or lose the Rat Race,
you are still a Rat!"

There must be change for growth to happen, with baby steps. *Hey, I didn't get that wound up overnight you know*. I'm consciously seeking out opportunities to change. I'm going to continue to work on altering the rapid cadence and stride that I call…. my life.

We have an infinite number of choices that we have-to/get-to make each day. How cool is that! We can explore our current modus operandi and ask ourselves;

"Is my way of doing things
truly serving me?"

It certainly is a challenge, yet I encourage and invite you to change one small way of doing something, ANYTHING every day.

Ask yourself, “Is the way in which I always do things effective and fulfilling? Does my approach feel good in my body and in my soul?” There is no time like the present to shake things up. Hell, if not now, then when?

Here are a few shifting prompts to help you begin the new adventure called…

CHANGE

SHIFT

Looking at my life as a whole in this very moment, I believe I need to change…

____

____

____

____

____

____

I want to change this/these things because…

____

____

____

____

____

____

By choosing to change this, I hope to...

____

____

____

____

____

____

____

All things notwithstanding, repeat after me:

"If it doesn't work, I ALWAYS have the opportunity to make another choice each day to come. EVERYDAY."

The changes made me feel: (i.e., excited, hopeful, curious, energized, a bit frightened in a good way, relieved).

____

____

____

____

____

____

____

____

____

____

Continue shifting, continue changing, continue growing!

Remember: Just like a healthy baby, everyone needs a regular change.

3

My Checking Account has $1.48 in it.

What a Relief!

It was such a beautiful fall day when I was out walking my dog, Ben. He routinely serves as my Thought Pondering Editor-in-Chief as we walk and talk out ideas. It's no revelation that the conversation is always one-sided, however thought-provoking for sure. While on our usual route through the neighborhood I suddenly stopped. There it was, a burnt dollar bill amid the fall leaves. Who would burn money? It isn't against the law? Maybe there is some mysterious story behind this barely-there bill? Am I on Candid Camera?

Picking it up, I quickly determined that it wasn't the elusive treasure that we all are dying to fortune upon. The buried coffee can of cash secretly in some long-lost relative's backyard somewhere in Timbuktu.

(*If anyone out there actually does travel to "Timbuktu", please send a postcard to the rest of us.)

It struck me powerfully as I picked up the burnt, barely-there bill to look at it closer. Were rituals performed at that particular location? *"The Burning of the Bills"*? Who knows, but what is certain is that it was laying there on purpose. For me to find. Or, so I thought. The money was burned from every angle, almost to the point of no longer being a bill. What little was left could not be salvaged, but the remnants of what used to be 1 dollar, 100 cents (or a daily wage for an unskilled worker in many countries) suddenly made me value what that barely there bill represented.

It seems we are always striving to enhance our individual lives, better our families, grow our business, be more, larger, better, richer and faster. This is all well and good and most certainly well-intentioned. HOWEVER, we trudge uphill with backpacks of burdens thrown over our shoulders in our quest to discover IT. The next big thing, client or destination of so-called success. Beating ourselves up daily in the process because we are never enough being just ...well,

NOT O.K.

The burden that we may feel of not ever really measuring up, we're never quite getting far enough or being good enough is so damn exhausting. This daunting heaviness doesn't permit us to pause and be grateful for what we have <u>already accomplished</u>. No, I won't go on some - sappy soapbox serenade.

I am pushing PAUSE at this very moment and I encourage every one of you to do the same.... simply **STOP**, just as I did that morning. Don't ask for permission. Don't feel guilty or sappy. Don't put it off. Just do it.

Having gratitude in our lives means not burning the candle at both ends to the point that we don't recognize our value - the blessings we have already created, the people that are blessed to be within our perspective worlds, the clients we have served, and the connections we have cemented.

Any human being that has been blessed by our talents, skills and expertise has in return, helped us to invest back into ourselves, our families or our work.

When things don't go well the human brain is wired to automatically default to what <u>didn't work</u> in our past as a protective defensive mechanism.

Instead, in this moment, can you pause and pick up the 'tattered dollar bill' and be grateful for it and what it represents? Instead of burning the candle at both ends seeking more, different and faster, I want to encourage you to think of a co-worker, customer or client to be grateful for; someone who has crossed your path or contributed to you in a positive way in the last week or month.

SHIFT

I am so grateful for…

because…

I, Kaari Allen, am grateful that you are taking time out of your busy world to read this because there is nothing more that I want to do than share my experiences and offer hope and healing to others through some of the pain and lessons I have been working through and still am **to this day**. You, the reader, are propelling me forward in my journey to live life to the fullest and celebrate positive momentum in this world we all share.

THANK YOU from the depths of my heart.

4

Eating Ice Cream for Breakfast

Don't Just Ask Why, Dare to Ask Why Not?

True success means asking yourself these four questions: Why? Why not? Why not ME? Why not NOW?
-James Allen

There they all were, every single beautifully adorned, enticing, seductive last flipping one of them. Each one just sitting there smirking at me. It was as if they were challenging me to give myself the green light and pursue one of them (or all for that matter)! After hemming and hawing and a lame attempt in devising some self-talk, psychobabble 'Personal Permission slip,' I finally surrendered. My hand slowly reached out toward them hoping that nobody witnessed this breakdown of will power. All bets were off....

Did I deserve to have any of them? Was I even 'good' enough to have even just one?

That scene rolled like this: there were three people ahead of me at the checkout that day as I waited in line at a local thrift store to buy a few romance paperbacks for my elderly mom. The location of the freezer with the ice cream sandwiches, frozen Snickers and Fudgsicles stacked up like little eye magnets was strategically placed just to dare me. I swear.

Why not have one for breakfast I thought? You haven't eaten yet this morning after all, I reasoned with myself...After spending WAY too much time rationalizing, I decided *why the hell not?* Really, would someone send me to the Principal's office? Admittedly, the amount of thought I had put into this verdict prompted me to start thinking more and more about WHY NOT?

Why the hell not?!

Why not eat an ice cream sandwich for breakfast? Heck, eat 2. Why not learn to play the guitar or even just go listen to someone else play one? Why not go climb a tree? When is the last time you went to a matinee on a Tuesday or went skinny dipping? If the answer is in high school, well... get out there and feel liberated for heaven's sake. Mind you, if you decide to skinny dip at the YMCA pool, there may be some push back from the general public. Truth be told, no one should really give a rat's rear hind what another person looks like anyhow. Think about it.

Personally, I hope the swimmers have much more exciting things to discuss than the amount of cellulite on the back of my thighs.

Why not do some things that you just want to do… just because you can?

Soon after I agreed to the *2018 Great Thrift Store Ice Cream Purchase Accord*, I would discover that I wasn't the only one asking this question.

Everyone asks themselves "Why?" but my friend and Director of Women in Networking, Teresa Thomas*, also dared to ask, "WHY NOT?"

Those two little words became the new mantra for me after learning about what Teresa dared to create for her own 50th birthday. How cool is this; she made a list of 50 Fun Things to do in a year. Given that there are 52 weeks in a year there truly IS enough time. The "I won't have time" excuse just doesn't fly. No permission slip required. No need to seek approval. No imaginary consent form for someone to sign.

SHE JUST FLIPPING DID IT!

SHIFT

Name at least one thing that you have been tempted to try, do or explore but haven't yet:

____

____

____

____

____

____

____

____

Describe some specific reasons you may be holding yourself back:

____

____

____

Think of just one step this week that will nudge you gently forward to make the above happen (i.e. tell a friend, make the phone call to sign up, research the details, allocate some money towards it).

My step will be…

Keep this in mind - there is no such *Board of Directors of LIFE* that determines whether each of us have permission to look ridiculous, or be child-like, or whether we can or should do something different. Quite frankly, if there were such a board, I can guarantee you, they are not having any fun and probably wouldn't serve any decent snacks or cocktails at their meetings either.

Go ahead, eat ice cream, skinny dip, get into your jammies at 5:30 like in 2nd grade and binge watch something on Netflix. Think of something that you have been yearning to do or are curious about, and take just one step toward something, anything, special this week. Our world today craves our participation as well as our unique contributions. Given the current state of negativity and fear that we all seem to live in much of the time, you owe the world the little joys of your own individual acts of courageousness.

Hold me accountable as well. I'll take a step if you will...

*A special thank you to Teresa Thomas. The world needs many more encouraging people like you!

5

I never really liked pie anyhow...

It Matters How You Slice It

Full disclosure, you can question my college roommates; I actually ironed my dressy shorts while they were on my person to save time before heading out somewhere. They remain some of my closest friends to this day, so apparently either they are insanely accepting. Or they just felt sorry for me back then.

I think I would rather dig my eyeballs out with a grapefruit spoon than continue to live like this.

Not prioritizing leisure, nor downtime, nor space to stop and take a breath and maybe read a book just for the hell of it? Full disclosure, at one point a few years back, I thought to myself,*" If I could only eat my breakfast the night before I go to work, then I could save time the next morning."* For what, more obligations, efficiency to perform our interminable laundry list of obligations? So glad that no one was privy to my unproductive, self-sabotaging self-talk…until now of course.

Yet, we are doing this to ourselves, day in and day out. Those of you who ARE NOT living like this, burning both ends of an ever-melting candle, please, please, for the love of God, conduct a workshop or lecture series for the rest of us to attend.

If doctors are accurate and we should get 7-8 hrs. of sleep each night, we have only 960 minutes of our waking hours to spend (given the 16 hrs. remaining after sleep).

Here is a breakdown of how we typically spend all those precious, once-in-a-lifetime minutes:

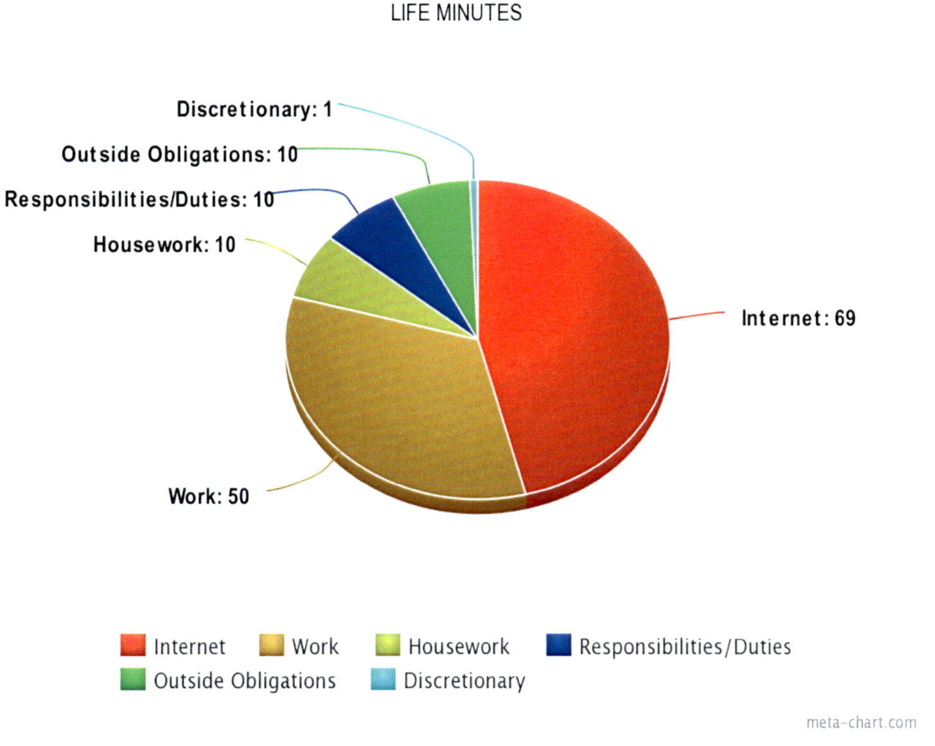

In each day, our waking hours equal only 960 minutes. Here is the breakdown of how we typically spend all those precious once-in-a-lifetime minutes:

50% Work
10% Housework[2]
10% Responsibilities/Life Duties
10% Outside Obligations
69% Internet (i.e., Media, T.V., Facebook, emails, shopping, games, etc.).
Clearly, much of that %69 media time is spent during the workday.
(as statistics state these numbers, I would venture to guess that many bosses are likely aware, if the job gets done. Most minutes are spent outside of work, but this statistic probably remains on the low end.)

1% Discretionary = 9.6 minutes

= 100% TOTAL

Wait, WHAT?! *# @&!

1% "Discretionary time... out of 100% of our day? Looks and feels like a complete blast of joy huh?
Have you ever pictured your daily life in a pie chart? Most likely not, but for the moment let's think of a day in our waking hours. These 960

minutes referenced above don't even include bathing, getting dressed, eating, using the restroom nor the time we spend driving "hither and yon."

Each one of us is only gifted one so called go around and this is how we are CHOOSING to spend it? Really?

There is a tradeoff once these minutes are spent...those 960 minutes, they are well, GONE. I'm no MatheMAGICIAN, nor scientist, but they are just gone, done, finished never to come back again, ever.

Something's got to give!

"Cut my pie into four pieces,
I don't think I could eat eight."
-Yogi Berra

Just as a side note here, my grandpa used to ask us kids where we had been...hither and yon? As an adult, I discovered that this is not the name of a place, which I always thought it was in my youth. (You wonder if they really did ever teach geography in schools back then). Anyway, the Merriam Webster Dictionary describes hither and yon meaning *"in various directions in a very disorganized manner."*
Somehow, this also describes portions of my day. Possibly yours as well?

Why do we feel guilty or strange spending time watching the sunrise or loving up our dog a bit longer than usual?

Stop and describe at least three things that truly fire up your soul; these may include, hobbies, interests, animals, athletics of any type, art, cooking, spending time with friends, music, etc.

1.____

____

2.____

____

3.____

____

Ask yourself, "Do the things that fire up my soul fit somewhere in those precious 960 minutes?" If not, they absolutely could. We cannot possibly give to ourselves, our families, friends or businesses if every sliver of our personal pie has been spoken for. AND, not necessarily in a way that fills us up. There will never be more than 24 hours in each day, but the cool part is that we can free up space and time by <u>choosing to prioritize a bit differently.</u>

“Truth, Liberty and The Pursuit of Happiness” …. our God given rights that were granted, enforced and protected by our governing founding fathers.

But, are we protecting these rights as sacredly as we could or should?

Admittedly, it is still a visceral challenge (not just a cognitive one), for me to simply sit during the day and read for pleasure for even half an hour. Years ago, my therapist assigned me, as homework, the challenge of sitting and reading during the day for pleasure. Yeah, I know…you could say I am a slow learner. Or she just likes to see me in her office routinely. I am not going to ask her which, I’ll just continue scheduling ‘tune ups’ in her office.

SHIFT

I invite you to try this along with me; Each day, even for 10 minutes, try taking:

- 10 Minutes to lollygag, meander or pause.
- 10 Minutes to watch the sun go down
- 10 Minutes to simply linger a bit longer at a shop, park, party or on the phone.
- 10 Minutes to merely sit on your butt. Heck lay down under a tree and look at the sky.

Try it right now… crop everything out – just like you would crop a picture on your phone for the best view of it. Simply sit. I know you can do it. You won't be 'wasting time', you will be replenishing your soul.

My soul needs even 1 hour a week to slice out time to…

____

____

____

____

____

Why does my soul crave this? Require this?

How could this potentially fill me up and renew my spirits? Change my life? My relationships, my overall health?

After choosing to do this, I feel....

____

____

____

____

____

____

____

P.S. Lollygag really is in the dictionary. My former 7th-grade boys made me look it up after I used it to describe their less than consistent on-time entrance into my classroom. Oh yeah, and 'dillydally' is too. You can do both, as long as you aren't trying to get to class on time.

6

You Can't Move Forward Using Only One Oar

Unless you would rather just go in circles.

Yes, I had another surgery, aka Functioning Enhancement Procedure (just sounds sexier than surgery). Due to numerous injuries, this was surgery number seven on my dominant hand and it required a final repair/enhancement to be performed. Trust me, I won't go into the mind-numbing and tedious details of the operation however, throughout this ordeal it brought me to reflect on the many research studies on the right and left hemispheres of our brain's and their distinct capabilities.

Any Google search will come up with a ton of research encompassing both the right and left hemispheres of the human brain. The right hemisphere dominates the left side of the body and vice versa. As you can observe in the illustration on the next page, the left hemisphere is responsible for our logical, mathematical and more analytical skills and the right hemisphere for language processing, creativity, and emotion. Suffice it to say, if the Good Lord had intended for us to recruit capabilities from only ½ of our brains, one would think he would have filled the other ½ with Bubble Wrap, Silly Putty or some other alternative filler.

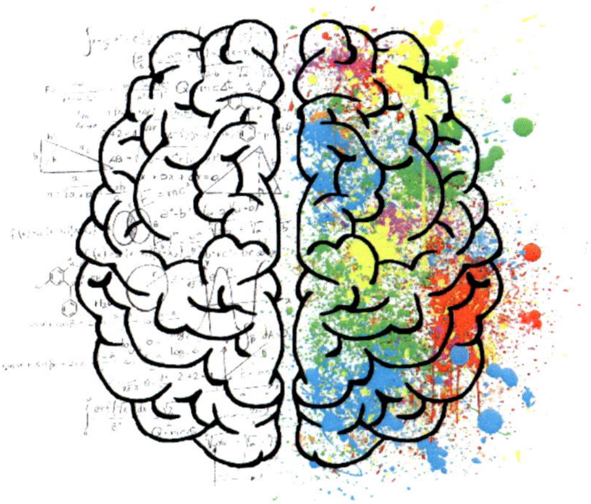

The challenges of my right hand forced me to learn a new way to open a bag of chips, cut my food or surrender and ask for help to carry, clean, to blow dry my hair. My attempts to hook leashes onto my dogs' collars using only my left hand while straddling them to hold them still is yet for me to conquer. I venture to guess that my neighbors get quite a kick out of watching me. Maybe the dogs will learn to do it themselves someday and possibly win a Canine Talent Contest. All other things remaining equal, we are simply working to complete the daily tasks of dogs and humans living and being.

Interestingly, this entire escapade thus far has masqueraded as a gift to me for many sundry reasons. This may possibly sound like some canned, Pollyanna rationale to you, but truthfully, knowing what I know and being forced to shift my entire world professionally and personally….

I would go through it all again.

No, really, I would. I'd just drink a little more wine along the way in the hopes of adding more levity. Albeit that I had to hold a glass with my non-dominant hand during most of my recovery, I might as well have made it more fun.

Neuroscience continues to confirm that we are to recruit and strengthen skills and functions from our ENTIRE brain. The brain is extremely malleable and has the remarkable capability to alter and strengthen weaker or underutilized functions. It is however, up to us to employ both sides. Not unlike a circuit breaker, there are synapses or "switches" that we can engage that help us function. Naturally, we gravitate towards those functions and strategies that are personally rehearsed and fit with our individual styles, personalities and affinities. For example, I dictated this as it is easier and more efficient. Yet, being somewhat right-brain-dominant, I was also dependent on my chicken scratched notes.

Each challenge strengthens our resolve and resiliency. We tend to remember what is difficult rather than what comes to us automatically. If you are more logical and analytical vs language based or creative, then taking an art class would challenge not only your right hemisphere but may also shed light on talents you never knew you had. There are also studies to indicate that we can possibly stave off cognitive decline due to aging by engaging both hemispheres to complete tasks. There's some good news!

"Life is about using every color in the crayon box."
- RuPaul[2]

7

Ski Wear & Pajamas

A Much Needed Attitude Adjustment on a Rainy Day

Exasperated and disheartened, I stood there looking out my kitchen window. Considering it had been the fourth consecutive day of gloomy, dark, wet weather <u>this</u> really had started to get to me. A self -defined "Outside Girl", I was tempted to grab that grapefruit spoon again as the rain continued to fall and the clouds hovered like a heavy wet blanket. The Ark had been capitalized upon long ago, so after my morning devotions a.k.a. Attitude/Approach Adjustment time, I ventured out and up to the end of the driveway. Stooping down to retrieve the morning newspaper, I became mesmerized with the dirty flow of water heading down the street gutter. Comprised of mucky rainwater, pine needles and a food/gum wrapper or two…not pretty. It occurred to me that all of this would eventually wind up heading towards some cesspool of sorts somewhere further along near a drain.

My neighbors must wonder about me at times and chat about it amongst themselves, but I give out really great Halloween candy. As I remained there watching the dirty, garbage laden water swirl about as it moved passed me, there was a choice I had to make. Either go with the flow so to speak or choose an alternate direction as I began my day. Mind you, I wasn't going to prop myself down on an inflatable inner tube and move within the current, but the gloom of the day certainly didn't help and I needed to do <u>something</u>. The tempest of negativity, fear, filth, and drudgery could easily grab hold of me and take me downstream right with it. I had to choose.

"Object in motion stays in motion until there is an opposite force"

-Albert Einstein

Reflect on a time when you were approaching an event, responsibility, conversation, or a complete, overall day that you were dreading. You were worrying about it and felt negative prior to it and you shifted your thought process in a more positive direction just to muster through it: (i.e. sitting through a lecture series on "How to Crochet an Afghan" with the gal you just started dating who is really into crafts.)

____

____

Earlier that same morning, I had planned on heading over to pick up my parents from their senior assisted community. I must share that it has truly been nothing short of gut wrenching to witness both of their various stages of dementia. Having always been very close to them and as the oldest of my siblings, I have assumed more of the direct care role simply due to where the three of us are in our lives as well as proximity. Thank the angels in heaven that my siblings are great and we all have the same feelings wrapped in different packages/ different roles. Even though the sun hadn't shone in days, and I had a laundry list of my own calls to make and to-do's and to-be's, I had to walk my own talk:

"Do it in joy, or don't do it at all."

(I created that mantra just to keep myself sane, or at least try to, about a lot of things.)

Preparing myself to take them to lunch that day, I got into my car. As I sat at a stoplight I made a choice, I had to. That, or it would end up being a very arduous day.

This precious window of time with them would never pass this way again, ever. Period.

Walking in, there was dear old Dad, sitting on the couch with a smile on his face….not always the case, trust me. "Hi", he said pausing to recollect who I was. He continued," How are you?" In his mind, he was *ready* wearing his blue striped pajama pants and his red ski parka, zipped up over his chin.

He then reached up to hug me. Albeit that it was 86 degrees in their apartment, he did mention that he had a 'little bit of a chill'. I've learned to dress in layers when I go over there. My dad has shouldered his Dementia with humor, grace and a lack of pride. Don't get me wrong, this is not necessarily the man of my youth, and there have been many trying moments in the past 10 years. But he has always willingly, accepted the fate of his slow demise and I can't even imagine how scary and painful that must be for him. On this day, he had proudly shared that he had been able to push the Big Blue Button on the automatic time telling gadget we had gotten him for Christmas. He hits the blue button and the very helpful woman robotically offers the time. It was $14.99 on Amazon, brilliant. Previously, we could conquer the gift giving with a new golf shirt for him. Unfortunately, not so much now.

One of the first faculties that is lost in those with Dementia is short term memory, processing, vision and the ability to read. I honestly pray for a cure in the future,

I can't imagine...

Dad stood up to start heading to the door to go out and announced, "I'm ready to go out, but we need to get Mom out of bed."

Being READY can mean any number of broad and variant descriptors for each of us by the way. My husband John would concur with this. He typically is in the car waiting for me to go; ... anywhere.

Eating lunch at Applebee's that afternoon with them, I thought about how easy it would have been to have gotten swept up in the cesspool of lamenting, worry and drudgery of that day. We sat there chatting and I offered some options on the menu for he and Mom to choose from. "Is that something I would like?" he asked innocently. "Yes Dad, that is something you/we have ordered before and you liked it." I said with a smile. Struggling to eat his soup with a fork and French fries with a spoon, I helped him and smiled. He was <u>thrilled</u> about his meal, being able to spend time with my mom and me and simply just BEING.

If only we could be that content huh?

This former less- than agreeable, impatient man of my youth, Division 1 college quarterback for Wisconsin and retired Delta Airlines pilot, was allowing himself to flow with his unfortunate circumstances regarding his health. He enjoyed simply the moment. I can tell you that he wasn't floating down the draining of negativity. My dad has no choice regarding his innate capacities nor the cards that he has been dealt. However, most of us do to a certain extent. A small tweak in how we anticipate and participate in daily circumstances can make ALL the difference.

SHIFT

Thinking back again about the situation that you previously reflected upon when you <u>chose</u> to alter your perspective/ attitude, what transpired for you?

____

____

____

____

____

How did you feel?

What did you learn or confirm?

Is there perhaps a situation or activity looming in your near future that you can chose to shift your 'lens' toward?

"Dreading things that haven't happened yet forces us to have to experience fearful and negative emotions twice."

It doesn't need to be that way. Life is challenging enough...

8

I GET to vs I HAVE to

"Replacing just one word can restore the soul."

Waiting far too long in the Wendy's drive through one day to buy and then deliver a Frosty to my dad, I found myself trying to talk my way off the proverbial frustration ledge that began to percolate in my head. My dad has been on and off in hospice care for the past year, as he is in the end stages of his life. He certainly doesn't ask for much and a Frosty makes him so happy. It is that simple. It just is. Then it came to me as I sat there in the exhaustive drive-thru line.

"You don't have to wait in this line you know. You GET to." I said to myself. Yes, I could be doing something I felt I needed to do or running around doing something I thought of as fun, but really, are those things more important than this? Not at all.

As I shifted just one word, my shoulders immediately un-hunched (most likely not a medical term, but you can imagine the visual). The crinkle in my forehead receded and my heart warmed to a calm. From a cosmetic perspective this was helpful, but it also affected me from a health perspective. My blood pressure slowed as I continued to just wait for the

next car to move forward.

Don't get me wrong, there were still five cars ahead of me in line and three behind, confirming that I had no choice but to wait with no exit option.

Instantaneously, just by replacing one simple word for another I felt better waiting for the next car to move forward.

When my dad eventually does pass away, I know that I will desperately wish that I could wait in that interminable drive-through lane on his behalf…. even just one more time. I'll eventually look back and realize that 'having' to pick up a box of Depends, pay my parent's bills on their behalf or take them out for a ride and an ice cream was/is one of the greatest honors of my life.

"I didn't HAVE to.
I GOT to.
I WANTED to."

Yesterday, or during this past week, I HAD to…

Try rephrasing it: Yesterday, or during this past week I GOT to…

Shifting our perspective takes practice and self- awareness. I'll be the first to admit, it requires daily self-monitoring of sorts. Forcing myself to think, "Oh, I 'GET' to pay the post-Christmas bills" is assumedly a stretch, but walking the walk is something that I want to practice along with you so here goes;

I don't have to pay these post-holiday bills, I GET to have purchased gifts with the money I have earned and want to share.

I didn't have to host family and friends this Christmas, I GOT to. I am blessed that I have them. And by the way, they CHOSE to spend their time with me. Or at least they acted as if they chose to and weren't forced.

My husband didn't have to shovel the driveway, he GOT to (it was warmer supporting him from inside the kitchen I'll admit), but he/we GET to shovel the driveway of the house we own that provides shelter when so many others are homeless.

Try this:

You don't <u>have</u> to go to work, you GET to work to feel secure, make a contribution and earn the opportunity to participate in activities.

You don't <u>have</u> to call an elderly a friend or long lost relative to wish him or her a happy birthday. You GET to brighten their day & remind them that they are cared for.

You don't <u>have</u> to bring your son/daughter to hockey practice or confirmation. You GET to take them and feel blessed to have kids when there are so many, myself included, who always wanted to have their own children.

I'll share some of my GET TO's;

I GET to parent the most wonderful step-son in the world and wouldn't trade him for anything!

I GET to be married to my loving husband. I also GET to pick up his socks occasionally when he leaves them as he is probably out shoveling the driveway of the house that we GET to call home.

I GET to share this because I hope that it propels you forward if even in the smallest of ways.

I believe that we all GET to live the life that we choose and deserve. Yes, you GET to choose YOUR life. Aren't we blessed, really?

SHIFT

After listing your HAVE to's, go back and cross out HAVE with GET… and see how you feel. See what transpires for the better.

My routine HAVE TO's:

____

____

____

____

____

____

____

You don't HAVE to turn the page, you GET to.

I truly hope that you continue GETTING to do many things in your life.

9

Make Sure to Celebrate Your Belly

Yes, YOUR Belly

As I stood at the drinking fountain filling my water bottle that morning a gracious server at the resort said, "Señorita, you don't have to do that yourself, I will bring you a glass of ice cold water with lemons and cucumber to your lounge chair in the ELITE section."

Now before I go on, I must share that my husband and I were generously gifted a trip to this resort in Mexico. This gift also included the upgraded ELITE status from our extremely kind and generous gift-givers. I admit that just using the word elite makes me uncomfortable because it implies that we are somehow "a select part of a group that is superior to the rest in terms of ability or qualities." - definition Google Dictionary

We were required to wear the signifying ELITE bracelets, use the Special Gold Color towels that are given to the ELITE Members (not Magic Carpet Towels that made my legs suddenly longer, my breasts larger, or my IQ higher, FYI). These special towels were found on the chaise lounge chairs in the specially roped off section of the beach marked ELITE MEMBERS.

My husband, John, turned to me as we were reading on those coveted lounge chairs and simply said, "I feel like we are the Star Bellied Sneetches." What?! For a moment, I had to chuckle as I recalled the story by Theodor Seuss Geisel, better known as the insightful Dr. Seuss. In that moment, we felt extremely uneasy and somewhat embarrassed, as well as sad. We weren't 'better' because we had those bracelets on, nor were we better for sitting on the special towels. They are TOWELS for heaven sake!

Theodor Geisel wrote "The Sneetches and Other Stories" published in 1953. These are coveted and renowned stories of tolerance, diversity and compromise. For those of you who may not be familiar, it is the story of a society who creates a hierarchy unjustly favoring those members who have stars on their bellies over those who "have none upon thars."

It is 2019, and sixty-six years since the brilliant Dr. Seuss published this and many other wonderful works that we all remember and relate to. Through his life lessons, he taught us how to engage with, as well as treat one another kindly. It is both confusing and difficult for me that today there are still those of us who feel marginalized in ANY way. That individuals can be made to feel less-than, either by others who self-profess that they are somehow 'superior' to them (Star Bellies), or that they do not know their own beauty, unique gifts, nor the value what they have simply because they do not see the 'star' on THEIR belly as well.

When have you ever felt less than, marginalized, left out or "not enough?" Describe the circumstance that made you feel that way.

How would you feel/respond differently now, knowing what you know?

____

____

____

____

____

____

____

Whether we were born with a star on our bellies (riches, power, talents, privilege) it is our God given right as individuals to be exactly WHO we are and HOW we are. Don't get me wrong, there are many, many days that I wish I were a little different or better than who I am, as we all do. I wish that I was richer, taller, thinner, more successful...

But think about this - each one of us is truly one in a billion, zillion, trillion. The odds of you being born as you are...? About 1 in 400 trillion or more! Think about that and realize that there is not a soul on the earth even remotely close to being YOU. Life is a flipping miracle.

YOU are a miracle!

Period.

Hear me when I say, there's never BEEN another YOU. There ISN'T another YOU, nor will there ever BE another YOU!

The next time you too wish you were taller, richer, smarter, faster, more successful, more this or less that remember, it is my hope that there will never be anyone convincing us to somehow assign value to one another or become different than who we are.

SHIFT

Name 5 ★ STAR Strengths/Affinities you have. Come on.....

(i.e., knitting, geography, welcoming others, generosity, making a mean peach cobbler).

1. ____

   ____

2. ____

   ____

3. ____

   ____

4. ____

   ____

5. ____

   ____

Just do YOU!

10

Like it or Not...

YOU, yes YOU are a Teacher

"Miss Simonson, Miss Simonson." (I wasn't married until my mid-forties. I won't gag you with the sordid details of my dating exploits/disasters.) "You have to come quick, it's Jared!" One of my students yelled from the hallway as he ran back toward my classroom.

It was 1998 and I had been teaching Middle School Special Ed for about 10 years. I had recently completed my master's degree in Learning and Behavior. This will soon prove to be ironic, by the way.

Picture Jared; curly brown hair, historically sweet, rambunctious with a few "challenges" both in and out of the classroom. As much as I liked this boy, there was never a dull moment as his activities entertained us daily. In the spirit of full disclosure, he was the catalyst driving our teaching staff to attend Happy Hour on a more routine basis as he matriculated through his middle school career. (Here is a thought; how about Happy Hour be conducted BEFORE school and not after to ease the blow of the pending day instead of recovering from it?) In any event, Jared asked for a bathroom pass and promptly left the room as he hadn't been particularly interested in our vocabulary review exercise that day.

After a good 15-20 minutes, and no sign of Jared, I sent one of my best 7th grade Junior Detectives to survey the situation and report back to Headquarters. That brings us back to the cries of Miss Simonson I mentioned earlier. In a panic, I found a male teaching counterpart and the two of us found Jared in the boy's bathroom screaming, "I didn't think that it would really work! Help me!"

We quickly deduced that Jared had brought Super Glue to school and had adhered his bottom to the toilet seat to see if it would in fact, really work.

I honestly wish that I was making this up.

Of course, Jared's mother received yet another phone call from me. But not before the E.M.T.s were called to remove both Jared and the toilet seat and load him into the ambulance to take him to the nearest ER. Meanwhile, there WAS that vocabulary test to study for, but that would clearly have to wait.

Jared's depth of curiosity for these types of things has probably earned him a coveted position within the FBI today. Jared, if you are out there, I hope this finds you happy, healthy and not adhered to any objects.

To be fair, I have to tell you, Jared wasn't the only one with a spirit for trying something new….

Back to 1975, I was in 4th grade. Always the aspiring creator, I decided to make cotton candy from Nestle Quick and REAL Cotton. With a little sugar, water and a few stirs with a big wooden spoon, I packaged the "confection" in Ziploc baggies and set up shop.

Business was slow at my stand in the front yard. I did manage to interest one neighbor kid in either a $0.30 bag or 2 for $0.50. Noting the obvious bargain, the naïve boy bought 2 bags. You may be surprised to learn that I was consequently grounded, only after the neighbor boy's mom had to take her son into the doctor for serious constipation. *So I'm not an entrepreneur, OK?* I learned. I learned that allowing the experts at the State Fair to sell cotton candy was a better choice.

Alright, spill it…

Describe a ridiculous, funny or otherwise memorable childhood event that you learned some sort of life lesson:

____

____

____

____

____

____

____

There really IS a teacher in All of us. As we shift or at least contemplate change in some way, it is important to be reminded of YOUR own capacities to teach another.

The newest teacher in my life is Robert Doyle. I met him via a trauma massage therapist that worked on my hand and neck. Robert is an incredibly knowledgeable, generous, inspirational and gifted athlete. He is 25 years old, and as an influential speaker, he empowers his audiences to see the opportunities and the power of living life as whole as possible.

Robert is paralyzed from the waist down. He has endured over 75 surgeries to date. Ambulatory until the age of 10, a complication from a spinal cord surgery caused Robert to have a stroke which unfortunately manifested in the loss of his feelings in his legs. He played on the Olympic gold medal winning Para-Olympic Basketball Team in Sydney, Autralia. He has taught me to celebrate the precious life that I have been given.

The most impactful thing that Robert has taught me to utilize are my unique gifts and talents, as he does with everyone who comes across his path. Robert teaches me to find the good in every situation and every person. He not only models this every day, he teaches others that life's ups and downs, twist and turns pave the way to living your fullest life!

SHIFT

What have YOU taught another person in your life to do, to be, to think?

- ____

  ____
- ____

  ____
- ____

  ____
- ____

  ____

Keep teaching and learning. You can enhance your life each and every day as well as those around you. You may want to exercise caution when using adhesives. I know I do.
Thanks Jared.

11

Elementary School Field Day

Living Up or Down to Expectations

"Hold your head high, you are an exclamation point not a question mark!"

Mr. Tonolli taught 6th grade and was one of my all-time favorites; the teacher... NOT the grade. He was one of the first people, other than my parents or other family members, who fostered the expectations that I had of myself. My colorful quilt is woven together of part athlete, academic, tomboy, girly-girl and creative. As a Rule Follower, I wanted to do everything right and always expected that of myself; as unrealistic as that was for a 12-year-old.

One of the closing activities near the last day of 6th grade was the clearing/dumping out of our desks. We also relished participating in the games of the coveted Field Day 1977. Please tell me you remember your own Field Day; tug of war, gunny sack race, water balloon toss and carrying the egg on the spoon race? Personally, determining what to wear always kept me up the night before and trumped any sort of 'athletic' preparation, for sure. It was the grand finale of the school year for Pete's sake! Oh, and we were dismissed for the summer on top of that. How great.

That year was both special but also somewhat melancholy at the same time. We were entering junior high that next fall.

JUNIOR HIGH

♪♪♪♫♫♫♪♪ ♪♪♪♫♫♫♪♪

(Insert dramatic musical score here for crescendo affect)

Mr. Tonolli required each of us to meet with him privately as a "sendoff" and serving as a short reflection of our past school year. Now, it was my turn. When I was standing by his desk waiting for his revered remarks as well as a goodbye of sorts he said, "Kaari, sometimes girls don't think they are as smart as boys. Don't think for a minute that you are not good at math and science, because you are."

This proclamation was quite progressive for the '70s, if I may say so. No one had ever offered their endorsement of me for any of those types of skills before. Okay, I had only been on the planet for 12 years at that point, but still. He then whispered in my ear, "You may want to lose the pigtails before heading to junior high." God bless the man for helping me not only put to rest the "look" that I rocked (in my own mind) every minute of every day since kindergarten, but he also unknowingly helped me avert the possibility of committing some form of social suicide that coming fall. I will be forever in his debt for that.

From that day forward, I told myself that I was not only somewhat creative as well as a reader and a writer, but that I could do math and science as well - to some extent. Forty-one years later, albeit I don't work at either NASA, Goldman Sachs, nor follow a recipe correctly, the belief that I can do math and science made all the difference in the expectations I have of myself. Just to be the best I could be.

All sorts of influences can challenge our view of the capacities we may have. There is every opportunity to have new expectations of ourselves – even without any outside, unsolicited opinion.

"We need the opposite of judging, assuming and marginalizing one another."

-Dr. Wayne Dyer

In one of his best-selling books, author and speaker on self-development, Dr. Wayne Dyer, shares a story about how outside forces can limit our abilities to pursue our best selves:

"In the 1960's, a teacher was given a roster showing the actual I.Q. test scores of the students of one of his classes. He was given a roster for another class in which the I.Q. column had been (mistakenly) filled in with the students' locker numbers instead. When the roster was posted at the beginning of the semester, the teacher assumed that the locker numbers were the actual I.Q.s of those students. The teacher taught to the individual 'number' of each of his students" not to the individual's learning capacities."

Therefore, this teacher unknowingly, imposed his own limiting belief about his students' potential. This most certainly impacted each student's own belief system that he/she had for themselves.

"After a year, it was discovered that in the class the students with the actual higher IQ score did indeed performed better than those with the

lower IQ scores. BUT, in the second class, the students with the higher locker numbers scored significantly higher than those with the lower locker numbers!"

My background as an educator edifies that an <u>average</u> IQ (Intelligence Quotient) score will fall within 85-115 based on standardized testing. Sixty-eight percent of Americans have average intelligence. An IQ of 70 or below, would be considered low. A high IQ would fall somewhere above 130.

So, for example, an assigned locker #78 in the above example would mean something a lot different regarding expectations in the classroom for this teacher and student than say, locker # 128.

This example of 'teaching by locker numbers' says so much about individual potential and how what you believe can affect who you become. Wow, if locker numbers can foster that effect on a person's outcomes, don't you think that we could back off and not expect perfection from ourselves or others?

We CAN expect goodness from one another and FOR one another. If we assume the best of one another and most importantly ourselves, then the reality that there is enough abundance of prosperity, happiness and wellness multiplies. There is enough joy and fulfillment to go around. Really, there is.

"What you think about you become."

- Buddha

SHIFT

What are a few "Pie in The Sky" wishes, hopes or dreams you have for yourself, either large or small now or in the future? (Remember, you don't need anyone else's permission, or approval. This is your life, who cares what *they* think?)

- ____
  ____
- ____
  ____
- ____
  ____
- ____
  ____

Now say to yourself…

"I have absolutely no idea what is going to happen regarding any of these."

That's O.K.!

Write down at least one surprising, amazing or unexpected dream that you wished had happened in your life.

____

____

____

____

____

____

____

I can do x, y, z…to begin making that dream come true for me right now:

____

____

____

____

Start right now, expecting good things from yourself and others. Your life is a movie and you get to determine the setting, the actors, and most importantly, the self-determined, happy-ever-after ending.

12

You Deserve a Break EVERY Day

If you are of a certain age, you may have seen or heard this vintage McDonald's commercial. This little jingle from the '70s may now start on auto repeat in your head - you're welcome. My point isn't about fast food, but it has a lot to do with cutting ourselves some slack for heaven's sake. Lots of slack.

The fact that you are reading this right now is a ringing endorsement in and of itself, you have made it through thus far. Sure, there have been bumps and bruises, tumbles and falls but you have made through even your worst of days.

Keep going!

Recently, my husband and I attended the funeral of Sunny, my dear friends' mother. And Sunny was just that, a light in others' lives. I have known her most of my life. Both of my parents are in the end stages of their lives so this day was particularly close to my fragile heart. I grew up ski racing with Sunny's sons, Tim and Paul, who are also very talented musicians, having recorded numerous CD's as the Brothers Frantzich. If you can ever see them live, do it. You won't be disappointed.

Walking into the visitation at the church prior to the service, I looked into the sanctuary and saw music equipment set up. There were two guitars on stands at the front of the church. "No way; are they actually playing at their own mother's funeral service?", asked my husband John.

The service was a beautiful testimony to Sunny Frantzich's life, and we all sang numerous songs that Tim and Paul have recorded. As they clarified for all in attendance, "This is by no means a performance by the two of us, but an invitation for ALL of you to join in singing the lyrics projected on the screen." Tears were streaming down our faces as they played and we sang in celebration and memorial of their mom.

Why I wear make-up at times like these is still a mystery to me. Well, I guess I looked somewhat presentable when we left the house that morning. Seriously, I couldn't even read from the bible at my brother's wedding years back because I started crying, overcome with emotion - and that was a very happy occasion! Presenting a former student of mine with an award? Forget about it. Clearly, I need to pump up the volume on my Emotional Threshold meter.

Over the past ten years, there have been many ups and downs in my life as I am sure there have been in yours as well. Many days we think our best isn't good enough. We didn't get ALL of the cleaning done, finish the errands we intended to run, or earned the money we wished we had by now.

How many occasions have you thought to yourself, "If I ever make it through this day, week, night" whatever it was? Guess what - you have made it.

Every day is a 'do-over'

Describe a situation in the past six months that you never thought you would get through:

____

____

____

____

____

____

____

Tim and Paul made it through most likely THEIR worst day thus far, I am sure. More than likely there will be many more sad days for them as they begin to grieve. But, somehow, they will make it through, and <u>so will you.</u>

Thankfully, no one is assigning Life Grades, but if they were, I'd give us all an A+. Speaking for myself, there have certainly been some F days let alone G+ or worse. Thank God there are only 26 letters in the alphabet.

Somehow, someway, by hook or by crook, you have made it through your toughest days. See, you have already made it through another 3 1⁄2 minutes - the time it took you to read this.

Give yourself a break today and celebrate the 99.999% of the days that you have made it through. Stop and look back at what you have endured, overcome, and accomplished thus far. Give yourself an A+ and swing through the drive-thru and pick up a Quarter Pounder AND fries for yourself.

Name 3 kind things that you can do for yourself this week: i.e. buy ice cream, watch that show, pick up flowers, buy that shirt you have been wanting.

1.____

____

2.____

____

3.____

____

13

Paint that Pig

and Let Your Light Shine!

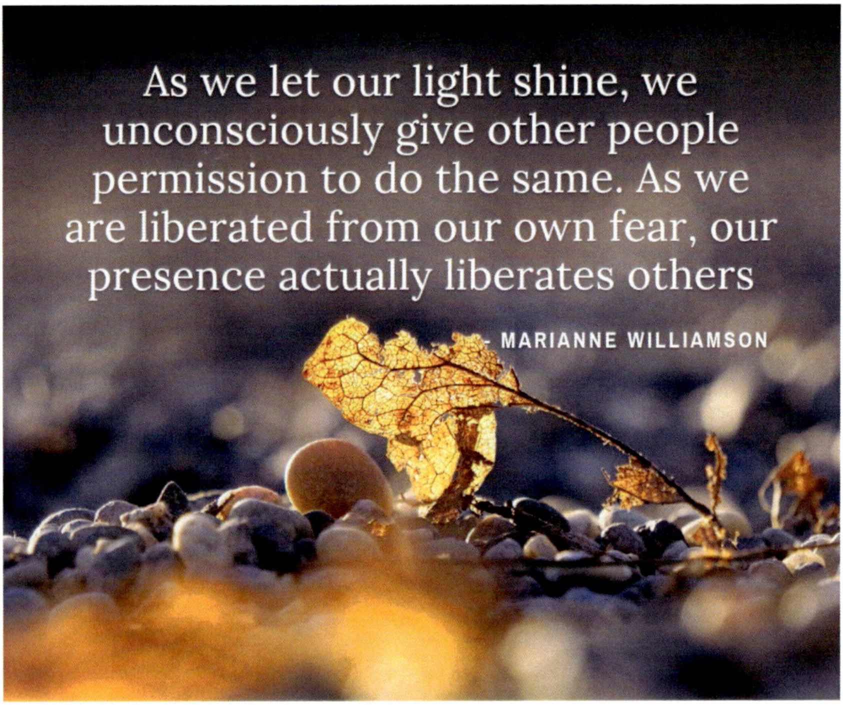

I was asked to speak to the occupational therapists of the Trauma Center at Regions Hospital at their professional development luncheon. Yes, 'trauma and luncheon' don't normally fall within the same sentence. These were the same highly talented, professional therapists that worked daily in a network of occupational and physical therapists helping me to retrain my dominant hand throughout six surgeries. Can you think of anything more enjoyable? Thank heavens these professionals made this otherwise very traumatic time in my life not only more tolerable but most importantly, healing.

Now I am placed in the position of offering coaching and healing inspiration from my otherwise outlandish personal and professional experiences; and now they vetted me to train THEM. What the hell?!

What would I possibly say? How could these therapists that have positively impacted my life benefit from me now?

Regions Hospital, Saint Paul, MN

As with many in the healthcare profession, occupational therapists offer amazingly skilled and compassionate service with little appreciation for their much sought after and vital efforts. As part of my talk that day, I asked them to privately write down 3 strengths or talents that they feel contribute to their team and or the patients in their care. I also required that they write a "secret" strength, talent or affinity that their colleagues would be shocked to learn of.

I know, I know, I had asked you to do this in the previous chapter... try to get over it and be with me here...

Silently laughing in my head, I was thinking maybe I was getting a little too much pleasure out of asking the therapists to write for me after all the hand exercises they had made me do (practice writing, etc.), in attempts to retrain my hand.

HAH!

After collecting their notecards to compile, I knew that I would then be sending this compilation of responses to the head of their department. Reading their answers later that day when I got home was fun and inspiring. Their responses were frank, humorous and REAL. It was who they were/ are. It was a treasure trove of the good stuff; the stuff that they were no longer going to be able to keep hidden. Even if it feels odd to boast a bit, it is better to share. Sharing and boasting are not one in the same.

Their collective whole deserved to learn of one another's individual gifts and talents. They were no longer going to just be "co-workers" who wore the same uniform; their sparkly stuff was coming to the surface.

The good stuff. Their best stuff!

Is there a positive something i.e. skill, affinity, trait, that you hide from the world because you are worried about being judged, laughed at or may feel self-conscious about? I invite you to describe it here:

____

____

____

____

____

____

____

The story I will describe involves a pig. I was coached to decorate a ceramic pig when I was hospitalized. Who knew that this was going to become yet another thread in the colorful and unique tapestry I call my life.

At the time, back in 2013, I was still in a hand brace after surgery. For my mandated occupational therapy, which I was not thrilled about at the time by the way, they required us to create something and join a group. The dreaded GROUP.

Curses, insert gag reflex here. Couldn't I just stay in my hospital room alone, reading People Magazine instead? Just as therapeutic, or so I thought. Fast forward five years.

I admitted to the therapists during my luncheon talk, that the mandated activity had dug up a lot of deep resentment in me because of my fears and the physical pain it would most likely cause.

What was I, five years old? Was that the first week of some kindergarten "Get to Know You" classroom team building?

Brother.

I was tempted to put three eyes on the stupid thing and paint it a putrid orange with big purple stripes.

The photo here is my resulting pink pig, sans the purple stripes. It now sits on my desk as a reminder of the perseverance to heal.

About a month after my talk, I received the highly decorated "Swine Creation" (on the right side of this picture next to mine) from those therapists via mail. It was a Thank You for inspiring them as both people and professionals. I was unbelievably touched.

My attitude has shifted tremendously since that fateful week in the hospital.

Now, my inner kaleidoscope has shifted and it has become clear that:

We should NEVER keep our gifts nor our interests a secret. Ever.

SHIFT

Have you ever felt broken by something? Ashamed of something? Not too proud of something?

How can you (or did you?) 'PAINT YOUR PIG' and begin to heal from it?

How can you/did you begin to shine a glorious light on a gift of yours that was eventually illuminated?

____

____

____

____

____

____

____

Shine on….. Shift on

And, paint your pig any color you darn well please!

14

The Potatoes Were a Complete Disaster...

but hey, I tried

"Failure is a bruise not a tattoo."

- Media Mogul Jon Sinclair[3]

There I was, an hour before the Thanksgiving Tribe was to arrive. And not unlike most of my ill-timed, hair brained ideas, I embarked on diving head first into this 37-ingredient, complicated, unknown recipe for 'Fancy Potatoes' that I found on the internet. Last minute of course. Yeah, I know.

My spin? You add on the descriptor Fancy, Jumbo or Deluxe to ANY object, experience or menu item and voila'! Before I go on, I may just add the descriptor Fancy to my name; "Fancy Kaari"...and see what transpires.

Presumably not a thing. It just somehow insinuates sophistication and coolness. Man, is that all it takes? What a cruel joke after all these years of trying way too hard.

Quite honestly, couldn't I have simply pledged myself to the idea of the good old tried and true Mashed? How did my culinary adventure turn out, you ask? My hockey playing nephews could have utilized them on the ice after dinner. I know that it didn't really matter nor impact the holiday, but it did feel a bit crummy that they didn't turn out.

Again, I tried.

Yes, it felt crummy. Yes, my Thanksgiving Tribe graciously choked those potatoes down without comment or fed them to one of the dogs under the table. At the very least it was a dry run prior to the preverbal higher stakes holiday cooking endeavor...CHRISTMAS.

(or maybe we'll just make a reservation somewhere instead)

An article in Smithsonian Magazine detailed the importance, yes, importance of failure. Without failure, there would never be innovation, sharing of ideas nor growth. The article, "The Strange Beauty of the Epic Fail", describes The Museum of Failure, which debuted in Sweden.[4] (There is also a Museum of Failed Products which makes its home in Ann Arbor, MI).

Curator, PhD Samuel West, details why the 140,000-item archive of ill-timed inventions, hair-brain ideas, and ingenious attempts at product creation gives individuals and corporations counsel for betterment and success. Maybe there could be a curated museum of all our collected failures (thus far) somewhere? We'd quickly deduce that yes, we are buffoons on a bus just simply trying to figure it all out in this life.

Here's a good one from the collection; remember Richard Simmons' Salad Spray invention in the late '80s? It certainly was a brilliant idea for its time. Simmons' conceptualized it in a society when we weren't yet participating in the health craze that we now subscribe to. The pace of society back then was a bit less demanding, so by extension, the quicker and finer salad dressing application couldn't be appreciated nor in demand as it would possibly be today in 2019.

Remember the Samsung Galaxy 7 phone? It blew up, and NOT in a good way. Those phones would start on fire! Samsung lost approximately 3.1 billion customers. Here I thought my Fancy Potatoes were a failure. At least my Thanksgiving guests at my house that day could resort to eating another dinner roll and drink lots of water instead. A company's reputation wasn't at stake. My ego would rebound.

70-90% of products fail the first shot out of the gate.

"Harvard Business School professor Clayton Christensen, notes that each year 30,000 new consumer products are launched—and 95 percent of them fail."[5]

As fun as it is or ISN'T at the time, failure is very good for us. Necessary in fact.

Describe a failure either big or small, that you have experienced in the past six months. We can all think of an activity, recipe, job, relationship, project...

____

____

____

____

____

____

____

Most likely, each of us could generate a list, and in turn, compile a small novel listing all our failures.

It is human nature to desire approval, accolades and gratitude. I thought my 'Fancy' Potatoes would garner some ego boosting feelings, yet...

Failure is a prerequisite to living a truly full life. Sure, our egos are hurt for a minute, but the sting subsides and we eventually embark on betterment. We bring to the surface the need for change, alteration or enhancement ALWAYS. If I listed all my failures, and reflected on each dodged bullet, moment of growth, or rocky stepping stone the list would be lengthy. However, without a doubt, I'm so thankful that I have failed in my life to get me to where I am today.

"The worst that can happen if I fail yet move forward, is that I move forward even in some small way."

Dig a bit deep, brush off your ego and delight in a past failure. In the true spirit of transparency, vulnerability and…eventual transformation, when you think about it, aren't you thankful it happened?

P.S. if you are wondering, and I really hope that you aren't, I will serve plain old mashed potatoes from here on forward. I'm o.k. with it and simply welcoming people into my home and well, I gotta say, my Thanksgiving stuffing sort of rocks. Full disclosure, it's out of a box but my guests seem to like it.

SHIFT

Try not worrying whether THIS or THAT will turn out 'right or wrong', 'good or bad'.

Describe something that you can just do and not worry about whether it fails or not:

____

____

____

____

____

____

____

Success really isn't the goal.

Living a fulfilling and happy LIFE is.

(regardless of how the potatoes turn out).

If you would like to learn more about the Museum of Failure in Sweden, here is a link to a fun video: https://vimeo.com/220999602

15

Welcome to Life Funeral/Celebration

a Special SHIFT Exercise

Wear bright colors- no black mourning outfit needed here!

"A bitter tree bears no fruit."

Matthew 7:17

A new season of your life and your world begins today... no really, it does.

Sitting there, bawling my eyes out in my former therapist's office, she looked at me and said, "Do you want to do what I did to get over something? i.e. *@!*&$ of an ex-boyfriend?" Of course, I said YES as I continued to suck my thumb in the corner of her office still in tears.

Kathy Hanson, LMFT now retired, was a very gifted therapist.

Thank you Kathy, you have single handedly changed my life.

She had me write out all my feelings, frustrations as well as the brain damage I was doing to myself and light it on fire. Yeah, like with a match.

Not being a believer in hocus pocus, I did it and it instantaneously freed up SO much toxic and ruminating brain and heart bandwidth, that very minute.

As I watched the ashes disintegrate on the sidewalk that day, I realized, that this negativity and pain was no longer welcomed in my life, nor took up space nor energy. It stopped consuming my thoughts.

Just buy picking up this book, you have made a shift. It takes courage to change. The exercise in this chapter is meant to bring you a chance to say what you need to say/ feel.

Why should you do this? Because you may have carried hurt, anger, betrayal, pain or disappointment. It needs to go, because it no longer serves you and it is holding you back from your best life.

Complete the next three pages and follow the instructions on page 139.

Dear ______________________________

(You choose person, event, regret, toxic situation, negative self- talk etc.),

____

____

____

____

____

____

____

I have been...

____

____

____

____

____

____

It is not ok for me that…

____

____

____

____

____

____

____

This situation is no longer welcome in my heart, head or world. I'm not living the authentic life that aligns with my truest self and desires.

I'm no longer going to…

____

____

____

____

____

I am choosing to move forward today ________________________________

(Today's Date)

These extra bags, a.k.a. "matching luggage" of toxic *$&!@ and suffering can't come along for the exciting and fulfilling life I am creating for myself.

I CANNOT WAIT to...

____

____

____

____

____

____

Thank you so much for the lesson. I release this for my higher good. It WILL all be okay - much better than I've ever thought possible. Because I deserve it!

With gratitude for how far I have come up until today.

I, (sign your name) ______________________________________, **am saying goodbye to this forever.**

Final Funeral/Celebration Shift:

1) Fold, roll or tear this funeral section out.
2) Determine a place that you can burn it… really burn it. Light it on fire and let it disintegrate in front of your eyes. (I've even been known to do this in a parking lot with clients and for my own funerals if a bonfire or fire-starting metal bowl isn't within reach).

Just be safe and choose a time that feels good and when you aren't rushed.

3) You can choose to be alone or share this ending and beginning in your life with someone you trust.

Doing this in my past has truly changed my life by letting go and freeing up space for positive change.

How do you feel now after having your funeral?

CHEERS!!!

16

The Pen is Mightier Than the Text/Email:

3 Simple Steps That Connect Us

I would always watch for them in college. The anticipated handwritten notes that my mom would write and mail to me, as well as my two siblings while we were away at college locations across the United States. (Every so often, she would throw in a $20.00 – Hallelujah!). Of course, it wasn't the surprise cash that was so special, albeit it got me through my financially-strapped college years. Her handwriting always made me feel as if I were somehow closer to her in proximity. It reassured me that I was loved, thought about, and that she had taken the time to connect with me. The note confirmed that I was a priority. Her hand had physically gripped the pen as well as the note with the handwritten words which were mine to cherish forever.

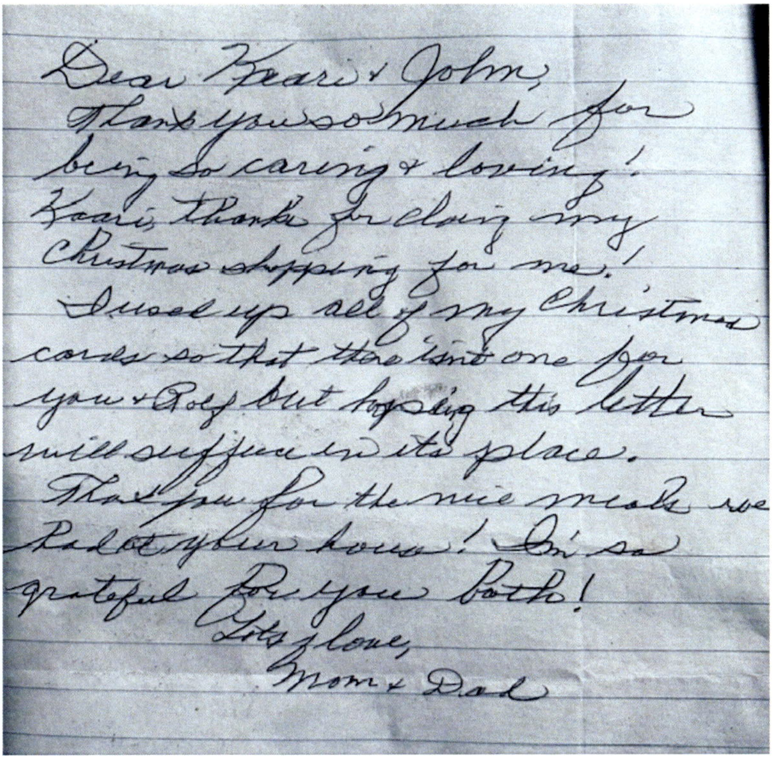

Dear Kaari + John,
Thank you so much for being so caring + loving!
Kaari, thanks for doing my Christmas shopping for me!
I used up all of my Christmas cards so that there isn't one for you + Rolf but hoping this letter will suffice in its place.
Thank you for the nice meals we had at your house! I'm so grateful for you both!
Lots of love,
Mom + Dad

The written word is so scarce these days. *Yes, I sound like some antiquated curmudgeon.* I'm ok with that. I don't have a bottle of ink and a quill nor smell of Noxzema cold cream. At least I am not hoarding Kleenex up the sleeve of my 'housecoat'. It has just always been a priority to me to write handwritten notes. One of the most painful consequences of all regarding the debauchery of my hand surgery was not being able to physically write. I still can't write/type for more than say, 10 minutes before I am in pain. My dominant hand is, well, "altered" if you will. So, I must ask for help; *NOT in my nature*, but the Good Lord knew that I needed practice surrendering to what I can and can't do. At least I am getting better at asking. The one finger peck with my left hand, not efficient but...

IT COULD BE SO MUCH WORSE

As a step-mom, I followed my own mom's example and wrote many short notes to my step-son. He and I hate the 'step' part as it implies that I fly around on a broom and he is somehow not 'officially' loved by me as much as if he were my own biological child. So, we skip it. He calls me "Kaar".

My mom would always leave a note so that when my siblings and I would come home late on a prospective night, we felt loved and encouraged. I tried to do the same for Ben. As the years went on and my husband John and my step-son Ben and I moved to our new house, I found them. In the top drawer of his dresser, there they were, this pile of my handwritten notes from me to him. It had touched him. Without telling me, I know that it meant something to him. Without a word spoken about it, he certainly melted my heart by having saved them. *(Hopefully, he didn't just choose to not pack them intentionally thinking they would be put in the moving sale with the dresser).*

When you receive an un-expected note from someone who loves or appreciates you, or was simply reaching out to connect, it is so special. Not an email, a text, a Tweet, a smoke signal or a Facebook message, but a.....

A REAL NOTE in your mailbox!

Amidst the credit card solicitations, bills and junk mail, seeing a person's writing on the outside of an envelope instantaneously creates connection.

Whenever I see someone else's handwriting, it instantly makes me feel more bonded to them. My husband knows that a hand-written note from him means more to me than <u>any</u> gift. (Hopefully he appreciates a note from me more than just the dreaded Husband To-Do list).

Three Simple Steps to Human Connection

On the next page is a removable Thank You Note template.

1. Think of someone that you want to share just how grateful you are for them and why you are grateful for them.
2. Tear out the page.
3. Write your note. It need not necessarily be that long if you don't want it to be. Then mail it.

SHIFT

Write your thank you note in the next week and mail it. Once you put it in the mailbox I'm guessing that a smile will come to your heart knowing that someone receiving it will know how you feel.

Remember, their response or lack thereof is of no consequence here. Just by writing it, you will immediately feel even more bonded with them

Dear ____,

Dear Reader,

There were many times that I wanted to give up dictating/writing this book due to all my hand surgeries and need for assistance, paying our own money for help and dictating etc., *(as well, as good old fashioned procrastination and then finally getting my 'butt in chair', as my editor says.)*

I want to thank each one of you for being THE reason that I finished it. I thought of all of you readers throughout the entire process. Honestly, my sole focus was to share my experiences as well as some of the ways that helped SHIFT me and propel me forward. It was the need to share the clearer and more colorful lens and perspective that I started to embrace about my life.

I thank you from the bottom of my heart and am wishing you all the best things in life. Most importantly, the most beautiful life that YOU choose to create.

Many Blessings,

CITATIONS

Chapter 2, Pg 25, #1 - N. R. Narayana Murthy Quotes. (n.d.). BrainyQuote.com. Retrieved May 3, 2019, from BrainyQuote.com Web site: https://www.brainyquote.com/quotes/n_r_narayana_murthy_704019

Chapter 6, Pg 61, #2 - RuPaul Quotes. (n.d.). BrainyQuote.com. Retrieved May 3, 2019, from BrainyQuote.com Web site: https://www.brainyquote.com/quotes/rupaul_818076

Chapter 14, Pg 126, #3 - https:/www.goodreads.com/quotes/4106140-failure-is-a-bruise-not-a-tatoo

Chapter 14, pg 127 #4 - Museum of Failed Products www.failuremuseum.com

Chapter 14, Pg 128, #5 - Professor Clayton Christensen https://hbswk.hbs.edu/item/clay-christensens-milkshake-marketing